The Fallacy of Freedom

By Gregory Heary

If people were naturally born with a love for freedom, people would have been fighting for it since the beginning of human history, but they haven't done so. Thus it follows that freedom is not something humans are naturally inclined to, rather it is a relatively new unnatural idea not found amongst our ancestors because they had no apparent desire for freedom. The humans of the past were not the idiots people assume them to be, they were humans just like us who had similar cognitive abilities. The main difference between present humans and the past humans is culture and technology. The humans in the past were not "too stupid" to understand freedom or to think of it. In actuality there is no right or liberty whatsoever which doesn't have an equivalent and corresponding duty to go along with it, as the price to pay for it. There are no free natural rights that humans have on earth, the world would not be the place it is today if one could get something for nothing. "Freedoms" are not free, they have a cost and in the past humanity did not want to pay the price. Contrary to what many countries claim, God has given humans the same rights all over the world regardless of their geographical position. Although these gifts and rights have strings attached. Not even God will give someone a free gift or privilege without expecting a "thank you". The one who receives gifts with gratitude is not equal to the one who receives gifts with indifference or disrespect. The responses we give to the gifts and blessings we receive from God can determine whether we get future gifts or not. God did not give the people in one country the right to speak freely and deprive the people of another from that same right. These are just claims countries have falsely postulated about God trying to make it seem that God favors them painting themselves as the best people of the world thinking their government was founded on divine principles instead of being created by politicians. This is just ethnocentric arrogance inspired by Satan, in order to disunite humanity making people feel God is unjust and favors some people over others because of something no one can control. Either God gave everybody these rights or nobody. There are no privileges which God gave to white people and not to black people, or vice versa.

However many countries throughout time have claimed God gave their citizens special rights, all this proves is that people lie about God. If you look at earth from a plane you cannot see national borders because they are invisible lines that were not geographically designed by God. Therefore it is impossible to see which land is trusting in God or blessed by him and which land isn't. If tomorrow all the national maps and borders disappeared people would just presume everyone had the same rights because we are all on the same planet belonging to the same species. As a result of this planet having one dominant species it is only fit that one organizational system works best. Unfortunately at this time the disunity of our species prevents such mass cooperation.

It is governments who tricked us into thinking God gives people rights based on their nationality or citizenship. As a result Satan has made God seem racist and unfair in order to make people feel God is unjust and oppressing them. This is why it is important to only take our information about God from his revelations and messengers, not satanically inspired government leaders or documents. If the prophets didn't say God gave man the right to freedom of speech and then some politician says that God gave man the right to freedom of speech, then that politician is claiming to be a prophet who is receiving divine revelation. The American declaration of independence claims the Creator gave man certain rights, the Creator did give man certain rights, but the authors of the declaration of independence didn't use divine revelation or prophets as their source of information when declaring what those rights were. They just made up those rights from what their own "intellect" and desires suggested, which could have easily come from Satan; especially considering who the draftees were. All the rights people have are only made known to us by God and his prophets. So if God didn't say humans have X right then they don't have it no matter how many humans later on say they do. A single human brain cannot think of what rights people have, nor can two brains, nor can every brain of all time and it doesn't matter which human brains think or conclude; they cannot derive what rights God has truly given us. Our brains don't tell us what rights God gives people, God tells us. If someone cannot prove God has declared people have X rights then you legally cannot say God has given them X rights. On a technical basis saying that God has given rights to people when he hasn't is a lie against God and is an act of disbelief.

The freedom of religion concept itself is a religious doctrine. Meaning that in order to believe people have a "right to freedom of religion" you have to believe in a religious dogma. To say people can believe whatever religion they freely choose or can practice whatever religion they freely choose is not merely a political/social statement, it is a theological statement and decree. "Freedom of religion" or lack thereof is a matter of religious creed that is a core component of theological importance effecting other beliefs regarding the afterlife as well as interactions with others during this life. For example if God says everyone can believe/practice whatever they want then how can anyone go to hell for believing or doing the wrong things? Wouldn't God have to make certain beliefs/practices illegal in order to justify punishment in the afterlife for people having those beliefs or practicing false religions? The answer is yes. And that is just one conundrum of believing in "freedom of religion" in that every other principle of a religious faith is affected by such a belief. In response some may say *"You can believe whatever but you can't practice whatever."* but you need to explain how that isn't contradictory and if one can't practice whatever faith they want then how can one say they can believe anything? So this is where these governments promoting freedom of religion are actually subliminally teaching a lot about religion and intricate interrelated religious dogmas. Knowing the importance and weight of such beliefs/statements forces us to verify whether any prophets taught the same or how they explained/reconciled a belief in future punishment for religious errors being justifiable if "freedom of religion" is something God has decreed or desired. Yet no prophet of God taught this and neither does any religious book or scripture ever printed, nor any non-religious text for that matter. The belief of people having "freedom of religion" (whether that's freedom to choose a religion or freedom to practice a religion) is a religious belief/ruling taught by a total of zero religions. Neither Judaism, Christianity, Islam, Hinduism, Buddhism, Jainism or any religions teach or allow "freedom of religion", or freedom to practice any religion of one's choosing. Every single religion in the world states that certain religions are illegal to believe in and illegal to practice, and those who do are to be physically prevented from either practicing or believing in them, and in some cases some religions decree certain religions are utterly outlawed and cannot be believed in, preached nor practiced with those who dare to do so being punished with severe occasionally life-threatening actions in this life. **In reality no religion in the world allows people to believe in any religion they choose and no religion in the world allows people to practice any religion they choose.** In practice neither does/has any government, including those who preach freedom of religion. Now for those who believe in any religion, which is technically everyone, it is impossible for them to believe in people having freedom of religion without disbelieving in their own religion. Even if your faith is freedom it is impossible to believe in religious freedom, it is a theological

9

impossibility because the doctrine is self-contradictory. To declare people have "freedom of religion" is itself a statement that forbids religions who teach opposing doctrines that forbid freedom of religion (whether in choice, in practice or both). Hence the doctrine of "freedom of religion" is incompatible with itself since if people have the right to choose their own religion then they must be allowed to choose ones which teach that there is no freedom of religion, yet they can't do that without rejecting the concept of freedom of religion. Therefore the freedom doctrine simply outlaws those religions, or certain doctrines, or as is the normal case people change their faith to assimilate within regions where "freedom" is the cultural doctrine labeling those who disbelieve in "freedom of religion" as either heretics or extremists for lack of belief in freedom.

The idea of "culture" was established in an attempt to find the dignity of humans within the context of modern science. Basically the concept of "culture" was invented to make people feel special and superior to animals without using religion or religious factors as the reason. This is because psychology teaches humans are nothing but brutes, yet everyone wanted to respect the dignity of man and still be "scientific" at the same time. Since religion had a bad reputation in Euro-merica they began to call it culture instead in order to replace religion with religiosity. That's why today if you change your religion many families will have little to no problem, but if you criticize or abandon your family's "cultural traditions" you might just get boiled alive. Some family's will say "*Oh your ancestors would be turning over in their graves if they knew you didn't keep their traditions going*". Most "cultural traditions" are the modern religious rituals. People will even say that "*If you want to marry someone of a different religion that's ok, but just make sure they have the same culture as you or else you'll have problems and difficulties.*" Religious tribalism has re-emerged under the name of "culture". However to have a culture means to think it's superior to all other cultures and hence every culture must advocate war against chaos AND all other cultures. That's why today they say it's a "clash of cultures" and not a clash of faiths, because secularists think a religious war is silly and wrong but cultural wars are ok and moral. Instead of "*converting the heathens*" they "*civilize the barbarians*". Yet since cultures got confused with ethnicities and nationalities, today what was once known as "faith" that later became "culture" is now called "values". In the West the word "values" replaced the phrase "religious doctrines". Although because false and incorrect "values" are not rational and not grounded in the natures of those subject to them they must be imposed by force in order to defeat opposing "values". Rational persuasion cannot make "values" be believed if they are false. Thus false "values" are never objectively debated because they'd get exposed as false which would cause embarrassment to those who hold them, and lead to cultural and political turmoil. Which is why you will find military force used to defend "values" and spread "values" because these "values" are false and incorrect. Essentially the Spanish Inquisitors were simply promoting and defending their "values" they just didn't have an issue with calling it religion. Since many today think religious violence is wrong they wage war for "values" instead. It's the same exact game, but nobody likes the stigma of the old name. Also this is because there is no concept of a "bad value", people say you either have "good values" or "no values". This makes a war waged to protect or promote "our values" automatically good and righteous to do, regardless of what those values actually are. There is no such thing as an "unjust war" waged for the sake of "values". However producing false or incorrect "values" and believing in them are acts of will. The reason people don't adopt false or incorrect "values" is not because of a lack of understanding it's because of their lack of will to have those false or incorrect "values". Basically they see those "values" as false and don't want them. That's why false and incorrect "values" are only spread through ideological war, economic warfare, military warfare and "cultural warfare". Or rather than "cultural warfare" today the term they use is "cultural diffusion". Many come right out and advocate "total war" without any prospective hope for negotiation because to negotiate in a war fought because of your "values" would mean to negotiate and change those "values". Always remember that "values" is the modern english equivalent of "religious doctrines". This is why you can tell most people you think they have a bad or satanic religion without them getting too offended at your opinion, because it's "just your opinion" but if you tell them you think they have bad/false/incorrect or satanic values they feel very offended. In the past when wars were admitted to be waged over religious doctrines there was always a chance peace could come by one side changing their religious doctrines, but thus far no people or nation has ever rejected their "values" and accepted the "values" of their enemy. So these wars for the sake of "values" might be the warhawk rhetoric for quite a few centuries, until all the bloodshed makes those with false and incorrect "values" see their "values" as less valuable. Therefore commitment is the equivalent of faith when God is replaced with self-provided "values". Which is why people started saying "*where there's a will there's a way*" because their faith is no longer in God but in themself and their goals. They become their God and those who teach them their "culture" or "values" are their prophets. Globally religion has not declined in popularity, the vocabulary and terminology used when talking about religion just changed. Religion and Culture/Values switched roles in society. All cultures teach their own type of religious creeds, some can be combined to overlap and complement each other while others will always contradict and conflict with each other. In short any theoretical "melting pot" can only have either pure water or salt water. This is because pure water and salt water don't mix together in the same pot despite both types of water being able to contain the same demographic ingredients when cooking various recipes for civilization. Likewise most of the creatures from salt water can't survive in non-salt water nor can most fresh water creatures survive in salt water. There are some creatures who can live in both, but most people cannot survive with 1 religion in a cultural "melting pot" with many various religions posing as "values". All values a person has comes from their religion, zero values come from a nation, culture, family, school, business, etc. If a person has values coming from multiple sources then either they have a religion which allows multiple values (but if they conflict/contradict that faith is false) or they have many religious influences shaping their individual custom composite religion. Every environment on earth is a religious environment, in our modern era we enter many poly-religious environments. Basically you might actually believe in more than 1 religion. Most people today do, unfortunately few of us ever realize it. So in some regards ancient polytheists were smarter than us because they knew when they believed in multiple religions. We tend not to know, but still live, fight and die for religions/values. While the fighting and dying may never end, our true religions and religious reasons should be recognized because if we don't know our own religions then our religion is ignorance. It is unanimously agreed that ignorance is not the true faith leading to paradise and true prophets didn't teach ignorance. We should have a faith that views human ignorance as sinful. Truly ignorance is the primary theological enemy of us all. Sadly for the majority of people religious ignorance is a value.

The guidelines given to American public school teachers in 2010 CE by the "American Academy of Religion" for how to *"legally and constitutionally teach about religions"* demonstrate how religious ignorance becomes a value. The 3 principles they are told to teach are: 1. *"Religions are internally diverse."* (Meaning every religion has many ways to correctly believe in it and practice it, there is no wrong way to practice a religion, it's about what you believe but then again all the religions have many diverse beliefs there is no absolute standard belief.) 2."*Religions are dynamic*" (Meaning every religion changes throughout time and is supposed to change throughout time and adapt to the times and places. Which means religious beliefs and practices of every religion are supposed to be different depending on the geographical location and the historical era.) 3. *"Religions are embedded in culture"* (Meaning all religions are just cultural inventions and social phenomenon, they don't come from God or gods or devils but are just cultural evolution. As such all of them must be respected because they are part of a person's culture and give us valuable historical traditions. They have nothing to do with politics. Historically they did but now we know that was wrong, unfortunately some extreme people live in the past and don't understand that different religions make society better by adding to its diversity. Anyways religion has been around too long for us to discard it, we'll just have to be tolerant and respectful so we can best use everything that each religion has to offer society.) Now of course this curriculum is completely abhorrent to anyone with traditional religious beliefs, but the teachers are taught how to delicately teach this to their students. The paper also taught how to respond to students who will object by saying *"my religion doesn't teach that"*. In such a circumstance the teacher is to respond by saying that many religions teach different things, so "your tradition" is different than other "traditions" in your religion, so you have to be tolerant and understanding that not everyone agrees with your opinions about religion, even if it's your own religion. The teachers were instructed that several beliefs denote a student with "religious illiteracy".

Two of them are as follows, "*Religious traditions and expressions are often represented inaccurately by those outside of and within religious traditions and communities.*" Meaning that if a student thinks that many people misrepresent their religion, especially those who don't believe in it, then they are "*religiously illiterate*". Secondly, "*Religious leaders and believers of a given religious tradition or expression are assumed to be the best sources of information about the tradition or expression and are often looked to formally or informally as "experts.*"" Meaning if a student thinks that religious leaders know the most about their religion then they are a "religious illiterate". It's the equivalent of saying that the prophets of God know the least about the religion God has ordained. Essentially the school teachers are taught to think the kids that think or say their teachers don't know what they are talking about are "*religious illiterates*" or "*stupid extremists*". Of course the teacher must never ever make the kid think they think the kid is a "religious illiterate" but they are told to be sensitive and confident that they are just overly passionate due to youth and "religious illiteracy". The public school teacher is told to teach kids they are the expert on every religion in the world and the "experts" are all stupid intolerant idiots that don't know what religion even is. To them religions are like candy, they all taste good and none are poisonous except for those extremists who think their attitudes are right/better and others are wrong/worse. This is where pluralism comes from where instead of the path to paradise being one it becomes plural. Secular school teachers practically don't know anything at all about any religions, because they couldn't in good conscience teach this stuff if they did or believed in one, however they pose as religious experts that know it all trying to make their students' passion and devotion to religion dissipate while making them think religion is simply cultural. That's the American curriculum and that's why kids in America often think a sin is "*Just a matter of your opinion. While just because you think the religion teaches X is a sin, it's not because religions are diverse and dynamic cultural phenomenons, not rigid or absolute truths from God or anyone special. Religions and sins are opinons.*" Public school teaches that religion is man-made philosophy. This is in order to reconcile religious people with the anti-religious doctrine of freedom.

At its core a promotion of "freedom of religion" doesn't teach freedom of religion but an intolerance of all religions that teach otherwise. The "freedom of religion" crowd at the same time they allege "freedom" are banning "anti-freedom", when they preach total religious tolerance they're simultaneously banning all religious intolerance. When people say all religions teach "freedom of religion" they are lying because not a single religion teaches that, such people are thereby subliminally teaching that if X faith doesn't teach freedom then it must not be a religion because they are defining religion based on the religious definitions defined by those who religiously believe in freedom of religion. Then you get copycat doctrines that evolved from the "freedom of religion" doctrine such as the infamous "No religion teaches hatred." nonsense of which again every single religion in the world teaches hatred for the others. Every single religion teaches hatred to such an extent that if I want to know what someone hates, I don't even ask them what they hate, I just ask them what their religious beliefs are and that's how I find out exactly what and who they hate. What this means is that the people who believe in or promote "freedom of religion" or the "No religion teaches hate." don't believe in any traditional religion at all AND don't believe anyone should be able to practice any traditional religion at all because every religion limits the "freedom" to choose and practice certain other religions and teaches hatred in a certain capacity for certain things. That it is impossible to find a person who doesn't hate anything is proof enough that there is no religion that doesn't teach hatred. Everyone hates something, and that hatred comes directly from their religion even if they don't identify their religion as a religion or as their religion. In conclusion people can make religious statements thinking they are general, neutral or even non-religious when in reality they are 100% theological beliefs that are religious in content and context. Sometimes people say stuff not realizing that doing so is to disbelieve in all religions, such as in the case of those who promote freedom of religion or denounce all types of hatred (particularly religious hatred). Then if you tell them they can't say what they say and believe in any religion simultaneously, they cite their "freedom of speech" and tell you that you can't say that they can't say something, again being entirely obliviously to the fact that such a statement is another religious doctrine/decree that effects or nullifies any possible belief in other religious doctrines/decrees taught by every single religion in the world. Therefore because so many people today teach and preach and practice religions without knowing they are religions, or preach and practice anti-religions not realizing they are anti-religions or anti-religious, we must carefully examine the belief in freedom to determine whether it's a God given right, a privilege, or a innovation from Satan.

There must be a distinction where there is a difference between freedom to speak the truth and freedom of speech in general. Not all speech is true, since lies are very dangerous Satan desires them to spread freely. After freedom of speech comes freedom of actions. Soon there will be people debating whether actions should have negative consequences, or if freedom should protect everyone who acts freely as they please. This has already taken

place in the realm of "Consensual Sex".
Initially adultery, fornication, homosexuality
and beastiality were crimes all throughout the
world. Yet in the wake of the sexual revolution
the doctrine that consenting adults can legally
do whatever as long as it is consensual
changed that. Why? Because freedom of
consent became so much of a cultural value
that it overturned the very order of sexual
society and will eventually lead to the
legalization of many formerly illegal things;
such as incest. Because there is no such thing
as legal precedent or legal consensus when
faced with the principle of consensuality. Yet
no prophet ever taught the principle of
consensual sin being made legal due to
consensuality. It doesn't matter what people
decide is legal in this realm, for our Creator is
the one who will recompense people according
to his own opinion and it doesn't matter how
many people vote against it. When it concerns
a command of God or a prophet there is no
room for personal opinion. One of the best
evidences against freedom of speech are the
countless dead bodies with suicide notes next
to them explaining that they killed themselves

because of verbal abuse. Rather than freedom
of speech there should be a duty of truth, or a
truth filter. Gossiping or backbiting cannot be
justified, even if what is said is true. Even
when it comes to the truth sometimes limits are
necessary. For example if someone is ugly you
don't go up to them and say, "*You're ugly*!", but
this is precisely the kind of thing freedom of
speech promotes, bullying. In that scenario it
might not even be true, in the opinion of the
Creator that "ugly" person could be the most
beautiful person in the world. It is important
to remember the etiquettes of speech whenever
we use our tongue because we will be held
accountable for everything we say. Freedom of
speech has no etiquette, no manners, no
morals, no respect and absolutely no duty to be
truthful or beneficial. The very reason more
than one prophet had to be sent to earth is
because people used freedom of speech to
distort their messages and God had to send a
new prophet to fix the distortions that people
freely choose to fabricate for their deluded
pursuit of happiness. Your tongue is a weapon
of mass destruction. It can destroy this world
and cause massive destruction to your

relationship with God and your subsequent afterlife. May we refrain from freely speaking evil and vain speech. If everyone used their tongue more carefully the world would be a better place. If no laws were made saying speech was free then it would be by default. Although once a law is made declaring freedom of speech then a gazillion lawyers will readily prove that "freedom" actually means this and not that, or that you cannot say this because of that. Therefore any country who declares they have freedom of speech actually has more restrictions on their speech than a country who doesn't claim to have freedom of speech. If you think a government has the power to give you the ability to speak, then simultaneously you must also think it has the power to stop you from speaking. No human or group of humans has that power. Don't think people died so you could have freedom of speech, even from a logical point of view only personal discipline can prevent you from speaking whatever you want, even if with a sword to someone's tongue they can still speak the truth no matter what any government says. Of course they might harm you for speaking, but they truly have no control over your tongue to make it say what they want. The primary reason soldiers fight is because they find themselves in a warzone in a life or death situation, oftentimes one they never planned to be in and it triggers either a fight or flight response. The other reason soldiers fight and the reason they frequently find themselves in a warzone is because they are getting paid. If they weren't getting paid they wouldn't fight, or put themselves in a life or death situation, unless they were suicidal. If they're not being paid money this payment could be the gifts God has given them, for attaining God's pleasure if the person fights for God's sake, the payment of peace of mind for the safety of oneself or one's family/friends, being paid with experience, for the anticipation of some type of payment, or for the payment of praise, fame or distinction. No one in the history of the world has ever fought or died for freedom of speech, because the only thing that can prevent it is one's own lips or divine intervention. It is physically impossible to fight for freedom of speech. Someone else killing another person has absolutely zero effect on the ability a person from a third party has in using their tongue. Do you really think if those people didn't fight then you would lose the ability to speak? God is the one who gave you the gift of speech! It is advisable to use that gift appropriately. It's a pity that people who have fought thought they did so for an intangible concept. The most they could claim would be to say they were fighting or killing so that they or someone else could be free from the consequences of free speech. People die every day doing stupid things, I sincerely hope no one else dies thinking they are fighting/slaughtering for freedom of speech under the delusion that it is something good or pleasing to God. Hypocritically the same people who promote freedom of speech would likely demand that these words be censored. Even after reading this some would say they're fighting/murdering just so I can have the right to write this. If that's the case please stop!

It's no coincidence that "freedom" is pronounced exactly the same as "free-dumb". The very concept of freedom of speech even goes against the rules of language itself. All languages have been designed with grammatical rules and restrictions that prohibit freedom of speech. Someone who wants freedom of speech essentially doesn't want to follow the rules of human languages. Instead of using human languages properly they think they can speak, write or communicate however they want to. There is no such thing as freedom of speech, because speech has rules which if violated means that whatever is spoken cannot be considered human speech. So someone who speaks with freedom of speech is not speaking any human language. If you speak a human language then it is linguistically impossible to have freedom of speech. Languages do not permit freedom.

Freedom fundamentally makes the option to do evil freely available. Therefore to fight for freedom is to fight for the availability of the opportunities of evil. This means freedom is fundamentally Evil. On the other hand God is the one who makes the rules and everyone has to follow them or face the consequences either in this life, the next, or both. Last time I checked God did not permit people to speak freely. Since freedom of speech nullifies the laws of God then it seems that freedom of speech was inspired to man by Satan. Understand that freewill is not a gift, it is a test; in fact it is "the test"(of life). Even when they are in Paradise people don't have "freedom of speech" to say blasphemy, lies, or insults. So how could people have it now? Always remember that in paradise you will not have freedom of speech, this is because it would harm other inhabitants of paradise and make it unblissful. Thus true bliss in this life is void of certain freedoms like speech. When people advocate freedom of speech just ask them why would they want something that is forbidden even in paradise. Anything truly good is present in paradise. Freedom is not present in paradise thus freedom is not good. Freedom means someone trusts themselves to know what's best. I'd rather trust that God knows better than I do or others. In order for us to follow God's prophets, and gain big profits in this life and the next, then freedom must be forfeited. The trouble is people want God to be their slave, not realizing they are God's. To have freedom means to be a sinful runaway slave from the Master of the Universe. Since all God's believing dutiful slaves retire to paradise when their shift ends, the *"road to freedom"* is really a self-paved road to hell. The free person is simply a slave of Satan and their own desires without realizing it. The difference is God lets people get away with their speech, deeds and beliefs longer than human governments do, but in the end the tongue, mind, heart, body and soul will be judged and sentenced for any crimes it has committed. So the "freedom", is more like the *"freedom of a criminal before they get caught, judged and sentenced by the authorities"*. Is that "freedom"? No, it's a temporary respite for a short time. You and I don't have freedom and never will. What we did, do and will have until we die is freewill and consequences. Freedom is a myth and false promise.

Many adherents of the freedom faith get told that freedom can only be defeated by force. This is false, violence need not play a role. Violence would only be needed if certain people supported freedom with violence as "freedom fighters". The only reason there would be "freedom fighters" is if they foolishly believed in the myth that freedom can be defeated or eradicated by force. Yet freedom can never ever be defeated by force, it's impossible. Such myths are used to enroll freedom fighters because freedom is a false religious belief and not a fact. Think of a believer in freedom as an undomesticated animal. No animal can be domesticated by force, such a thing has never happened. Every domesticated animal became domesticated through voluntary submission and a change in their beliefs. They all individually chose to believe they were not to be free, but owned by someone or something. Likewise a free animal can never be domesticated into a civilized person except through a change in belief and their voluntary choice. So this religious war need not have violence. I don't want violence and violence will not win this war; it could perhaps win some battles but never the war. Also keep in mind that action is different than violence and violence does not mean people get hurt. For instance Moses used violence when destroying the golden calf which people were worshipping, so violence is not always bad, nor against humans and is sometimes necessary. Also violent harm to humans is not always bad either as proven when David killed

Goliath. Yet these prophets didn't win their wars through violence alone and it was not their first resort either. Some prophets didn't even use violence at all, with others God used violence on their behalf, as in the cases of Noah and Lot. It is simple, refutation through true proofs defeats all falsehood. This is what the prophets taught.

Godwilling such false religious beliefs about freedoms have been refuted by my "*free speech*". What's that "*free speech*"? Yes, that is my definition of "free speech", in that I ask you for no reward or compensation for this message. When I offer speech or writings for free that is true freedom of speech. That is the type of freedom of speech Islam teaches, in that you should not get paid to teach people about religion. The only one who can pay you to speak is the one who gave you the tools to speak, the ability to speak and the job on what to speak, when to speak, how to speak and why to speak. God can pay you for it or punish you for it. Thus beware and if you are smart you will be silent more often. The wise people don't use too much saliva. What we speak or write will never truly be free, even if we don't charge people for such activities. This is because when we speak or write we are making an investment in whatever we communicate. That investment will either result in a good deed, a bad deed or a waste of time, thought and effort. Our speech is never free, it's just another aspect of the test of life. So be polite, not poetic, say what's right, don't be rude, your verbal utterances are converted into spiritual food for your provisions in the afterlife. Thus get points today for what you say instead of spewing/brewing poison you'll later regret, when one word can block you from paradise or put you into hell. It costs us something to communicate no matter what it is we say, thus the price must be worth it for us to let our tongue play, because the potential risk of speech is too great to pay. Thus what better thing to do with your tongue than to pray to the one who made your tongue in the way the prophets taught us in the language in which they taught us? Afterall since speaking is such a precious gift then surely the language you are speaking must count for something. You can actually get extra points if you speak the exact prayers the prophet taught. Also if we speak the language they spoke then we might start thinking the way they thought and acting the way they acted until we meet them in paradise and have a great conversation. Wouldn't you like to meet God and tell him you prayed using the exact words which his prophet taught? Plus if you were to learn the prophet's language and you don't know it already, you can intentionally learn it without learning the bad words so that way you'd protect your tongue from evil if you became fluent and comfortable in that language. Imagine not knowing bad words at all, you'd have a very clean mouth with a very clean tongue. Don't think it's too hard or impossible for you to do. The Creator made your tongue, and can help you learn a new language too. Silence is also a great language to learn and master, if you can.

Lastly there is a popular religious slogan of, "*Sticks and Stones may break my bones but words will never hurt me.*" Most people will think this is just a popular saying to help kids cope with verbal abuse via an optimistic placebo outlook that relies on the Santa Claus methodology of words only hurting you if you believe they can hurt you. Yet such a concept is not "just a saying", it is a religious doctrine used to validify the religious doctrines of freedom of speech. Words can and do hurt, a lot. Sticks and stones can hurt too but words can hurt more and cause permanent damage. Now most people would agree that if someone is using sticks and stones to hurt another they are guilty of one of two things. Either it is a justifiable act of violence, possibly as a part of warfare, or it is a sinful crime and a violation of human rights or even possibly animal and/or property rights. Therefore we have laws restricting the usage of sticks and stones where if they are being used illegally to violate the rights of humans, animals or property such criminals get stopped and punished. On the other hand we know that words are more powerful than sticks and stones and are weapons used in warfare just the same and can be used for both good and evil. However because of a religious devotion to "freedom of speech" people think it's wrong to have laws punishing those who use their words to violate human rights, animal rights or property rights. This is completely unfair and unjust to do. As a result the only way they can make everyone okay with verbal criminals being left unpunished is to promote religious slogans like *"Words will never hurt me"*. Everyone knows this is a false belief though, usually even when they hear it the first time. Typically a kid gets hurt by words and complains of the pain to an elder only to be briskly or compassionately told that *"No. Words will never hurt you, just remember the saying next time, you'll see."* Whereas any rational kid should immediately say, *"No I'm quite certain that words can hurt me so you are wrong. Don't lie to me. Even if personally I ignore the words, such verbal abuse can still damage my reputation throughout society and hurt my job prospects, marital prospects, friendships, interpersonal relationships and mental health."* Therefore by our societies being afflicted with the false freedom faith, we tell lies in order to justify our gross irresponsibility to stop verbal crimes and verbal criminals. Face the facts, speech is very dangerous and there has to be some restrictions on it. Unfortunately because in the past oppressors, the leaders of false religions, and the enemies of truth have restricted speech because of personal opinions now many in society think that freedom of speech is a better alternative than letting people restrict speech. However we have more than those extreme options. #1. I agree it is wrong to have people restrict another person's speech and forbid them from saying things. #2. It is wrong to let anybody say whatever they desire without facing legal consequences for their speech. So how can we have the perfect solution where evil speech is eradicated yet differences of opinion can be simultaneously expressed. The answer should be obvious, we just ask God what we can say and what we can't, then follow God's rules for punishing those who violate his rules regarding speech. Yet therein lies a fundamental problem in that many people disagree on who God is and what exactly are God's rules. Although the specific legal problem to solve for this is simply what are God's rules for speech? We can learn this by learning these rules from the most recent prophet of God. Muslims say this is Muhammad and we have a codified legal system. Nobody else has such a legal system, but they arrogantly disagree and say they don't want Islamic Shariah without even knowing the rules of it. Yet the thing is people don't have to be Muslims to use and benefit from Islamic law. However religious people know that to admit the Islamic law is better than their religious laws, or anything they can come up with, makes a very powerful statement regarding Muhammad's claim to be a prophet of God. This is because it's impossible for anyone who isn't a prophet to come up with a legal code that is superior to one which came from a genuine prophet of God. Thus non-Muslim and unislamic societies decide to stay stuck with misery and oppression that comes with the "freedom faith" because to abandon the freedom faith means to look for an alternative solution. Whereas since looking for an alternative solution to "freedom" requires examining Islamic Shariah's solution, then because such an examination would result in Islamic Shariah being objectively chosen as the best solution, this search and selection of alternatives to freedom never happens. In contrast enemies of Islam know that they can never abandon freedom to choose something else; unless Islamic Shariah where to cease to be an available alternative. Hence we have the modern conflict between Freedom vs. Islamic Shariah. Of which freedom of speech is a pillar of the "freedom faith", which has many different denominations particular to each nation which incorporates it with, or adopts it, as their national religion. So Islamic Shariah vs. Freedom of Speech is a important battle in this religious war. Whereas because I'm a Muslim I must side with Islamic Shariah for religious reasons. Now maybe you don't side with Islamic Shariah or think there is a better solution to freedom of speech. However because freedom of speech is so harmful to society and our species, even if you don't accept Islam or Islamic Shariah, on the basis of mankind alone you have to admit and accept the fact that freedom has got to go. Freedom and freedom of speech will destroy us all, mentally, emotionally and spiritually. So even if you don't want to support the Islamic Shariah solution, you should still actively oppose the false faith of freedom. Theologically, irrespective of which religion is correct, the false freedom faith is abhorrent to the Creator of the Universe. A person cannot be on the side of freedom if they believe in any other religion. So unless freedom is your religion and the thing you think will save you from the hellfire and get you a place in paradise then you must fight against the false freedom faith. This is because to believe in freedom is to disbelieve in God's rights, God's laws, God's prophets, God's revelations and God's punishments. Now don't misunderstand me using the word "fight" to be "fighting words", as I explained before violence is not desired nor needed. Yet one must think of this as a religious war because without God's help one can never win, even if they defeat their enemy. To win is to win the internal battle inside yourself, the external battle is the one where the enemy is to be defeated. Don't mistake the external battlefield as the most important one. If you personally don't believe in freedom and live a life without freedom then you win your war. But if you lose your personal war then you will be a loser in this life and the next even if you theoretically achieved victory on the external battlefield. Freedom is an invisible idol of arrogant "independence" and irresponsibility. Thus it's an easy idol to destroy since it doesn't exist. So I suggest you get this idol out of your house (if possible), out of your life, out of your mind, out of your heart and off your tongue. As with other idols, freedom is defenseless. Yet because it's an idol the only way freedom can ever be promoted is via lies, myths, traditions, legal threats, intimidation and violent compulsion. Thus there are freedom fighters who wage war for the sake of their idol. Not all of these are violent, unfortunately some of them are. Which side do you fight for in this war against idolatry?

If freedom is an option and opinion then why do so few today believe it is a theory? Why do people in "free" countries have such intolerance toward people who disbelieve/refute "freedom"? Is it just a political philosophy or something more? If freedom is not a religion then why have I read the proponents of freedom proudly declare *"freedom is more sacred than any religion"*. How can something be more sacred than a religion if it is not a religion? Wouldn't that make it more religious than religion or denote a type of super-religiosity? If we theorize that freedom were a faith and that some countries believed in freedom and others didn't, then how many heretics or disbelievers in freedom exist in those "free countries" where the majority of the population believes in freedom? In such "tolerant free countries" how many people disbelieve in, reject and are publicly free to denounce the concept of freedom? And if they do what happens to them? Do they not get treated as if they had disbelieved and rejected a religious doctrine? Are they not treated as a treasonous apostate teaching blasphemy? How can freedom be an obligatory belief which everyone in the world or the West is expected to believe in, without anyone labeling freedom as a religion? Because for freedom to be classified as a religion would mean it is a contradictory false faith, in that freedom is ideologically forcing people to believe in it through pressure rather than merit. If there is any type of penalty or stigma associated with opposing freedom, disbelieving in it, or denouncing it and offering an alternative belief, then that means freedom is an intolerant religious belief that is intolerant of all other religions. The problem with freedom is that it doesn't allow people the right to disbelieve in it or try to eliminate the belief in freedom. It is a tolerance of everything except for intolerance of anything, such as tolerance for everything. Freedom is intolerant of the opposing religious views that say the religion of freedom is wrong and false and should not be believed in, practiced nor applied in any legal system. Usually advocates of the freedom faith don't allow people to disbelieve in, doubt or renounce their faith of freedom. Freedom is a contradictory bigoted faith that feigns tolerance but is actually more intolerant of other religions than the intolerant religions are. To further test this theory of freedom being an intolerant religious faith of crazy fanatics, we can simply look at the prophets of freedom and see whether they allow people to disbelieve in it. Do they? No. As their pseudo-prophet Francois Voltaire famously stated, "*I disapprove of what you say, but I will defend to the death your right to say it.*" Which means that they don't give you the choice of having freedoms. If you say, "*God said don't take his name in vain, swear, gossip, backbite, lie, or slander so I don't have the right to do that.*" They will say you do have the right to do that and God can't tell you that you can't say what you want and they are willing to fight in order to force freedom upon you, whether you like it or not and whether God likes it or not. Meaning they will fight God for telling you that you don't have the freedom to say or believe or do as you please. If you tell them that God said freedom is forbidden then they say they got to kill that terrorist who is oppressing you and telling you what to believe, say and do threatening you with eternal and worldly punishment if you disagree or disobey them. The lovers of freedom believe people have the right to disagree with and disobey God without any consequences. They fight so people can disagree with and disobey their Creator and think they are heroes for doing so and expect gratitude as if they were holy warriors since according to them "*freedom is more sacred than any religion*". All freedom fighters are fighting against God. The prophets of other religions would've fought against them. Whereas the mainstream man-made faiths incorporated this heresy of freedom into their own since it made it okay for them to lie and lies are how they can spread their faith. Thus not every religion takes a stand against the faith of freedom because of its use to purveyors of falsehood. Current religious wars are more of a threat to religions than they were before because previously battles were waged over religious theory/doctrine, but now they are waged mainly over religious practices/implementation. Today the religious wars are waged against entire religious systems while the doctrines are frequently ignored. This is a more severe type of warfare because it doesn't matter what you believe in if you aren't practicing it. To believe is to practice, thus by stopping those of another religion from practicing they are effectively crippling the belief without having to win the battle theologically. Essentially the way the religious wars are fought today any religion can win, truth has little to do with the outcome. Presently there is no such thing as peace when it comes to religious warfare as there was in the past. Previously when the militaries were at peace the war was paused, but today peace does little to affect the theological combat and frequently the military peace treaties amount to pivotal theological battles. One thing about modern religious warfare is certain, most of the battlefields are no longer places of violence and the peaceful soldiers need to be more committed to the cause than the violent soldiers. Also the theological war is ongoing in every location every second. As important as the physical military battles are, now it's the peaceful battles that determine the outcome of religious wars. The believing soldier of truth never sells-out, yields, relents, conforms or flees from the theological battlefield. Because the soldier of truth has already surrendered, as a slave to the Creator. All prophets taught people they have to become slaves of God. Slavery existed in most of those eras and people knew what a true slave who totally submitted was like in how they thought and lived. Those the prophets preached to knew of slaves who didn't have total submission and they knew of slaves who did. The human slaves may have changed the ways they submit to their human masters today, but God's slaves always submit the prophetic way according to the prophetic definition; til death. Free people burn in hell. The unfree slaves of God go to paradise.

Unfortunately you will find creatures who claim to have a "free mind" and promote "freedom of discussion" or "freedom of speech", are not willing to even discuss such matters or consider them debatable despite claiming they are free independent thinkers who "*think for themselves*" and "*don't believe what they're told*". Thinking such things is blasphemy or insanity to them. Yet because they believe in freedom of speech, they will say you should be glad you are in their country where you can think and say whatever you want because of freedom of speech. They don't give you the freedom to debate many things, the notion of the doctrine of freedom most of all. They don't give you the freedom to argue against a free society or freedom itself. Yet how then can you really have "freedom of thought" when many subjects and ideas can not even be talked about with people or given any publicity? They may reject pop culture, because it's such a popular thing to do, but most all of them have a pop mind which is very narrow and only comes in the flavors available and allowed in their nation. Such is the tyranny of the disease of staunch devotion to non-conformity and "independence", which instead of resulting in true independence creates societies that are dependent on everybody because of their delusion that they can be free from depending on anything for their beliefs or from wholeheartedly submitting to the decisions of a minority. All they have is fictional freedom from the label of not being free, in reality they are mentally unfree even more than those who admit to not have a "free mind". A "free mind" is an empty mind which instead of being molded by oneself or a select minority it gets molded by everybody and anything. Thus rather than being ruled by one master of their own personal choice, they are ruled by a mob which they don't choose and cannot even identify let alone break free from. But since true free minds result in unstable ever-changing mentalities and economic/social/political chaos, this causes all alleged democracies to always become ideocracies that can't reform. The illusion of freedom is then used by a state as a buffer to prevent the true ideology of the state from being identified or countered. Thereupon such an ideocratic state can get away with oppression undetected with any formidable opposition. The only way to reform an ideocracy is to abolish it's beliefs, ideally this would come about through peaceful refutations. Wherein victory against an ideocracy can only come about through a mental/spiritual warfare since ideas are unkillable. Yet then they'll think and say you're brainwashing people. To which you can tell them that you can't because you ran out of all your brain soap while washing your own brain freeing it from the pollution which they are currently polluted with. Freedom is basically the shampoo modern ideocratic states use after brainwashing people to prevent others from cleaning their minds from the poisonous filthy ideology of the ideocratic state. Any who claim to be a "free thinker" is just ignorant of who their slave master is, which makes them twice as much a slave than the one who admits they are not a "free thinker". A "free thinker" is a foolish student thinking they were never taught anything by anyone and that they are unbiased, which they hope and claim to be since they are led to believe being biased is bigoted. But that they think they are a "free thinker" shows they are not and are deeply biased already thinking that a "free open mind" is a good thing when a "free open mind" simply means it's cheaper than cheap because it doesn't retain anything of value that enters it. A theoretical "free mind" is one that simply hasn't made up it's mind and is confused as to what to think/believe and is afraid to believe in something other than the idea of freedom being salvation. God did not create minds to be free but to have a program. The brain is hardware that is designed for certain software. God sends prophets with the correct ideas to put in our heads and hearts which should be accepted and installed once we are certain of the legitimacy of the prophet and the authenticity of the information as having actually come from God via one of his prophets. To desire freedom of thought means a person doesn't want to install the prophetic program in their life. But if one is living life then rest assured the brain is running on some type of program that has been installed into it, and if it's not the prophetic program then you will have problems in this life and the next with your relationship with the Creator of your brain. The test of life is that you pick your program. Yet everyone alive is living according to a program whether they picked it or not, because you can't live without one, unless of course you are brain dead. So the choice is you are either brainwashed or brain dead or you choose to let God brainwash you and install the prophetic program in your mind, heart and soul. Everyone's brain gets washed, whether one accepts the bath or not the soap we use is the only difference. So whether you call it soap or software your mind is washed or installed with either good stuff or bad stuff, some dirt or malware/viruses may remain or creep in from time to time, but your brain is not a "free mind" and you can never be a "free thinker" even if you try. You and others (like your parents, teachers, friends, family) already programmed much of your mind, but the programs we have in our mind at this time might not be the prophetic kind. The goal we should have is to pick/install the prophetic programs and avoid/uninstall/delete the devilish programs. So rather than "brainwash" the goal is to upgrade the brain. Just align your mind with the intended designs of the mind-maker. Don't listen to me, believe what the Creator wants. I'm just sharing what's in my mind so your mind might benefit. This book is a shared experience in that our minds are spending quality time sharing/learning information. If you change your mind about something that's okay if not that's okay too, depending on what it is of course. If something I write is wrong then don't believe it, but if something I write is right then it'd be wrong to reject. The only rule you should have is to side with what God wants, not with what you already think or what I think, but what is right and true. I'm just saying every mind is programmed. The powerful mind is the one which knows when, how, why, by who and what it was programmed with and chooses to improve itself. Your mind has already been made, but you can make it better so as to make your relationship with the mind-maker better. God did not create your mind to be free, instead God created your mind so it could be very valuable. A valuable mind is expensive, a "free mind" is worthless. Your brain cells are worth much more than money, how much more valuable then is the real estate of your mind? Think carefully about what you think about because you have a limited amount of time to think and limited brain capacity, your brain is always recording and deletes things to store memory. Thus be mindful of what you fill your mind with at all times. Your mind can either be a mine of beneficial knowledge or a minefield set to destroy itself. No two minds are equal and no two people are equal. Most brain damage is self-inflicted and pleasurable. The goal is not to have a "free mind" or an open mind but a healthy mind. The healthy mind is biased and knows it is biased, but despite the bias its willing to change it's opinions should it's opinions be proven wrong. The changes the healthy mind makes is based on the prophetic program and/or for truth. No human mind is 100% right about everything nor 100% healthy so we can always improve for as long as we live. To believe in God and worship God correctly requires a certain mentality, it's not just a feeling, thought or action. One needs the right mindset to properly believe and have that belief lead them to live their life the correct way. Our minds' have a setting God wants it to be on but sometimes we have the wrong mindset. Your brain is a tool which the prophets of God taught us to use correctly. Since you always use it, you can only avoid sin if you use it the right way. God will judge us for what we use our mind for. One of the best things to use your mind for is to express gratitude to the Creator of your mind for giving it to you. So what do you think of such ideas? The correct answer you should give is *"I think what God would want me to think of that."* but it's easy to say that without the statement being true. For you to obtain a believer's mindset this can never be done with "brainwashing", because filth will always enter our minds since that is what Satan does with his life. You could obtain a disbeliever's mindset by brainwashing but never a believer's. A believer needs mental hygiene from self brain-training. Some could help you train your brain sometimes but most of the training depends on you and what you do with your mind that God gave you. To think about the way you think and the reasons why and what you think about is to train your brain. But what are you training your brain for? To run a marathon? To fight a war? You should train your brain and heart so the way you think and the things you think of please God. Pleasing our maker is the purpose of life while freedom goes against our natural purpose. So may you be a slave of God as long as you live not just in thought, but in belief and actions as well. This book is just about the evil of freedom, others exist on serving God; which must be read if you are sincere in your search for complete blissful liberation from the shackles of freedom.

www.ingramcontent.com/pod-product-compliance
Lightning Source LLC
Chambersburg PA
CBHW011232120626
46549CB00008B/3237